Star Cat

Harting C of E Primary School
Tipper Lane
South Harting, Petersfield
Hampshire GU31 5QT

Carl went to bed.
Carl's cat Dora went to bed too.

In the night ...

... Dora went prowling in the garden.

Star Cat looks for buns to munch on.

She zooms up high!

Star Cat floats across the town.

Can she see buns in a shop?

No!

Can she see buns on a high speed train?

Zoom!

No! That's absurd!

Soon, she spots a stack of buns.

But a moon cow has got them!

Boing!

Burp! No food for you!

Spoil sport!

No buns for Star Cat!

In the morning, Dora slips back in.

Flip!

Flap!

Dora has a nap on Carl's bed.

Carl has food for her.

You must get up!

Carl's cat food is not as good as buns. But it is not too bad!